FIRE STATIONS

A. B. Jackson

FIRE STATIONS

ANVIL PRESS POETRY

Published in 2003
by Anvil Press Poetry Ltd
Neptune House 70 Royal Hill London SE10 8RF
www.anvilpresspoetry.com

Copyright © A.B. Jackson 2003
www.abjackson.co.uk

This book is published with financial assistance
from The Arts Council of England

Designed and set in Monotype Ehrhardt by Anvil
Printed and bound in England
by Cromwell Press, Trowbridge, Wiltshire

ISBN 0 85646 363 9

A catalogue record for this book
is available from the British Library

For Edward and Molly Jackson

Acknowledgements

The author would like to thank the editors of the following magazines, in which both early and finished drafts of these poems were first published: *Chapman, Spectrum, The Dark Horse, New Writing Scotland, London Magazine.*

Nine poems were published in *Anvil New Poets 3*, edited by Roddy Lumsden and Hamish Ironside (Anvil, 2001).

'Saturday Night' received a commendation in the National Poetry Competition 1999.

Contents

1965	11
Feathers	12
David Hume Considers the Moon	13
Night Work	14
The Christmas Pet	15
Arthur's Seat, Edinburgh	16
The Sleeping Gypsy	17
Parting on Henry Street	18
Schopenhauer's Porcupines	20
Stammer	22
Stratheden	23
Maryhill Road	24
X	25
Blackbird	35
Phineas Gage	36
Journey	37
A Ring	38
The Dancing Serpent	40
Acoustic Mineral Wool	42
The Blue Nile	43
July Fugue	44
The Temptation of Saint Anthony	45
Missing	49
Saturday Night	50
Beast of Burden	51
Lauder's Bar	52
Filing	53
The Silken Road	54
The Chemical Wedding	55
In Memory of R.D. Laing	56
Star	59
NOTES	61

For the Electrical fire is the spiritual substance,
which God sends from heaven to sustain the bodies
both of man and beast.

CHRISTOPHER SMART, 'Jubilate Agno'

My poor friend Smart shewed the disturbance
of his mind, by falling upon his knees, and saying
his prayers in the street.

SAMUEL JOHNSON

1965

The egg ferments, the one cell splits in two:
again, four: again, eight: sixteen: thirty-two.
Droplets of fat, like miniature dabs of butter,
nourish and sustain. Welcome, morula,
little mulberry . . . free-falling, spineless,
until, upon the uterine surface,

touchdown. Transparent, semi-opaque, solid,
the heart comes to fruition, big as a head.
Welcome, tiddler, mild water-scorpion.
Gills disappear, cartilage becomes bone.

Full term: seismic waves, electrical storms,
the twelve-hour haul of not being born,
between two worlds—induced. I make it late,
this bloody, headlong drop towards the light.

Feathers

Strong, precarious spirit, I will do
housework for these gifts: your sonic boom
of laughter shaking door-frame and timber,
the tenement crucible we now share.

Desires meld; pituitary glands produce
a Molotov mix of grace, adrenal sulphur.
And if I saw Edinburgh all ablaze,
an angel etherized in the dead

bird you held up, struck road-side, I'd say
love's accelerated or made us crazy.
Pianos play some New Jerusalem boogie . . .
bells of St Giles . . . the feathers in our bed . . .

David Hume Considers the Moon

*No human testimony can have such force as to prove
a miracle*
AN INQUIRY CONCERNING HUMAN UNDERSTANDING,
1748

Compare the two: a goose feather, a town.
Breezes blow. Imagine the *town* airborne.
The chance of such unearthly violation

is next to nothing: truth is uniform.
The heart is weak. Testimonies run
so counter-clockwise, and with bells on—

wonders hailed by many, *seen* by one,
and that one prone to weird internal song.
We cannot, then, allow this other kingdom.

Yet even now, with Physics in full bloom,
our masters wax alchemical: Newton
ploughed his groundless magic, vague *mysterium*,

concocting holy God within a stone.
Mercury is poison; salt goes with ham bones;
that is that. Forget the flaming dragon.

If seas could part, if any son of man
could preach his low-born gospel from the moon,
a world's undone; our nature, sorry bedlam.

Clouds will burst with rain, not pears or plums.
Miracles make a mincemeat of reason.

Night Work

after Roberto Juarroz

As I sleep, my two hands come awake
and work their craft, create or unpick
some halfway human body, stitch by stitch,
play Frankenstein all night behind my back.

I hear them, from my sleep: I hear them groom
this bastard demi-ghost, this bloodless *golem*,
doctoring its life, its other death.
I wake, with two hands folded on my chest.

The Christmas Pet

A blood-sport refugee
kicking its heels in sanctuary.
It was an impulse buy,

spurred on by the children
and the straw season.
Care required, minimum:

recommended food, anything,
make the den inviting,
give the gold nose-ring

a good polish.
It did not flourish:
I offered barley and mash

without success. It grew
lean and repetitive, slow,
lean and repetitive. Now,

having churned up the lawn,
it patrols
the small circle of indoors

scoring things with precise horns.

Arthur's Seat, Edinburgh

The night air carried nothing of the city;
the sky, a slate grey-blue beyond routine
bankruptcy, the government of loss.
Blackbird, rattling its thicket, had no
ear for trumpets. Spring intuited itself.

What sank from high dark to horizon, stone-in-
water, escaped all newspapers and the day's
thin infatuations: a canopied ring of lights
hovered there: ghost-carousel, UFO:
the Blackford Hill observatory. Come dawn,

an ordinary world returned: dew on bracken,
a team of painted, fire-forged horses
dropping like stars from the sun's womb
to carry off a crowd of shoeless children.

The Sleeping Gypsy

Painting by Henri Rousseau (1844–1910)

My best dream came
and found me as I slept
It came
on four legs with a heavy head
Its ribcage rose and
fell it came so
soft it broke my heart and held me
small within its eye
It stood outside my sleep I could not see it
It had no words to say but knew my scent
It had no words to say and would not wake me
I woke when the moon had gone
and my dream
whose mercy is my sorrow

Parting on Henry Street

You're close, you're very close.
So say the Minotaurs of love,
oiling our vanity.

Dublin's a maze, the sea
its only solution.
We're deep in Henry Street,

some cut-price durable
goods emporium,
stuck for an exit.

*The spinal column ends
at eye-level.* Your eyes,
a petrochemical blue;

our fall from sense
a Buster Keaton comedy:
twenty storeys high

and swan-diving, our progress
broken by one
awning after another, each one

stretched, pregnant with body weight, each one
bursting its
bubble and so on

down, until we shatter
an entire city.
Signboards, mesh and steel

float off. You and I
lock horns in the dust-cloud,
unharmed, unholy,

staggered by tenderness.

Schopenhauer's Porcupines

why should you want any other when
you're a world within a world?
ELLIOTT SMITH

I

This is the world I recreate: your teeth
weakened by cane sugar or stomach acid,
the ripe avocado-garlic of your breath—
whatever tottering truth our kisses hold,
nine hours down in drink, or body warmth
brought slowly to overspill in this bed

overshadowed by monkey-puzzle trees,
a spiked climate, resisting any grasp—
look: our bloody life line, the palm's crease
punctured as we come and freeze and gasp
the tongue-tip Christian name of Jesus.
This darkness was our first night, and our last.

2

Porcupines amble through midwinter,
disturbing fern-leaf and fallen pine cone.
Topsoil turned permafrost, a ground zero,
survival hangs on huddling together.

And suddenly—it's hellish, being close,
reciprocal prickles all they ever share.
So, they squeak and flinch from each other,
taking their slim chances with the cold.

Elastic retreat: again they come together,
again cause injury. It's what they know.
A central self-sufficiency is the goal—
or so said the unwed philosopher.

Stammer

Dear larynx, Venus
fly-trap of a throat,
spit it out—

your sticky food,
the words
'innocence' and 'Icarus'.

Telephones are dangerous.
My sound is pure
howler-monkey,

vocalising high
in the green canopy.
How exotic!

It's ridiculous.
My first name stalls
at 'A——,' a dumb horse.

So who, to wit, who?
Dear Coherence,
thank you, goodbye, thank you.

Stratheden

James has wet his pants, and frowns.
He sniffs his fingers, looks at me, grins,
accepting the smell as a gold prize.

Tom is waving his hairless arms.
As always, I ask him: *What's in your box?*
Chocolates? Fruit? And off he trots.
I speak like Miss Jean Brodie here.

William swings, and cuffs my ear
while hosing-down his daub of shite.
I dress him roughly, pull on socks
too small for his feet. I watch his fist.

One Sunday a month brings visitors in.
Some hushed-up boys may recognize
their mumsy daughters, their lost wives.

Maryhill Road

19A   Milngavie   1 min
19A   Correction   2 min

ELECTRONIC BUS–STOP DISPLAY

I will wait the extra minute
and go to Correction
where sweet peas grow upright
on the lawns of Eden

where light-adjusted children
play safe in the dark
all sugar no medicine
their games unelectric

where groups of identical pig
make perfect bacon
where men remove garbage
and work the oven

I will wait the extra minute
and go to Correction
to catch the unwavering scent
of brimstone

X

Ten studies for the Christ-figure

I do absolutely understand what Giacometti meant
when he said to me, 'Why ever change the subject?'
FRANCIS BACON

We may guess or imagine anything we like. What
shall I say, Lord God?
ST AELRED OF RIEVAULX

I   IXTHUS

A mere glyph,
a glitch.
A wag of tongues.

Battle charm.
A fresh worm
to bait Leviathan.

Ghost-born,
his bones
numbered to a man.

2   LETTER TO MY SISTER

St Aelred of Rievaulx, 1160

Sister, for your comfort, I'll say this:
our good Lord lactates upon the Cross,
his breast unbuttoned. Suckle. Ample grace
will half quench, half stimulate such thirst.

Comb rough linen; stitch a wedding dress.
Observe your wooing Husband, arms outstretched
in one unmelting offer of embrace.
His wounds, kiss; your lips, turn scarlet lace.

Guard your cell, remain forever chaste;
resist, as I resist, all men but Christ,
sweet myrrh, beloved . . . Sister, as I write,
trees compose their fruit, sparrows nest.
Spring is here, at last: the River Rye
a constant froth of copulating snakes.

3 THE MAN OF SORROWS

Petrus Christus, c.1450

Half-dead and fresh from your bed chamber,
your side-wound a palpable vagina,
bloody, offered open, your crown a tiara
twisted from peacocks' tail-feathers or flowers,

what on earth are you? The heavy lidded eyes
reek of hashish, the pear-shaped figure
of some hermaphroditic brothel-keeper.
Mediaeval Christ, yourself. It's no surprise:

whatever crime was consummated there
with you the blank slate, the virgin bride,
remember: men at root are polarized,
switching from snow-white to pure terror;

their gifts, the long-stemmed orchid and the sword,
a pornographic pin-up of a god.

4 THE SLAUGHTERED OX

Rembrandt van Rijn, 1655

The church road
lined with blood-pails,
butchers' blocks.

The liturgy
bursting with infallibles: cut
this way, this artery.

The nave
consecrated with tannic acid.
Skinners' Day.

My god
rotating on a spit.
The tough inedibles

ground down,
my credo: *feed
the living with the dead.*

5 THE YELLOW CHRIST

Paul Gauguin, 1889

Scarecrow—your skin
sun-cracked chamois leather—
bless me now.

Christ, citrus—
tell me the word grows.

6 BELA LUGOSI

(1882–1956)

Who, in his Hungarian youth, was Christ,
leading some backwater Passion Play.

The photographs are uncanny: his hair
in ringlets, immaculate centre-parting,

the Scourging, the garden's Agony. Later,
Hollywood's black pantomime, his Dracula:

garlic-shy, flinching from the Cross:
eternal life contracted with a bite.

7   CRUCIFIXION

Francis Bacon, 1933

X-ray plate, radiograph, resolution poor.
Image unknown: pin-head bat, the Lord
Jesus Christ in flight, musculature
and mirage, sperm-white, ectoplasmic trace

of slug slime or god-presence. Pilgrim, catch
those ribs unhinged and floating to the right
for they are his: dwarf star detritus, relics
flung from orbit, mixed with all, star

breakdown, meltdown, holy—holy—holy—

The Cross: a saddled horse. It threw me.
Not clear, not free: with one ankle trapped
in its stirrup, I dangle upside-down—
arse over tit, some Christ-comedy.

Birds land on my foot-sole and sing.
Blood rushes: inches above my head,
a grassy, worm-infested earth,
the amplified scrabble of creation.

Whatever I carry—grief, small change—
drops from my pockets like spring rain.
This flipped vision: a single elm tree,
branches buried, roots in heaven's ground.

Prehensile Lord, between you and me
there is always some god almighty
animal playing gooseberry,

its breathing
laboured, deep-sea, its head
laced with injuries.

And I remember—
that holiday trek, a boy
too high on his first horse,

fear-dazzled and saddle-sore,
pulling up short before a
half-ton black

bull which guarded the gate ahead.
Back in Brodick, fried cod with vinegar,
crazy putting while midges bit.

Between you and me
the Minotaur—

Mother of All: I taught her well
and whispered, *Know me, know yourself.*

My father was a jealous type.
I forged my kingdom, tooth and nail.

In desert sun I turned to bronze,
the Christ original, raised on a stick.

I was the last to kiss Cleopatra:
she ran to me hot from Antony's bed.

Today I shed my final skin,
unlock my jaw, preparing to swallow
the egg whole.

Blackbird

Summer.
A blackbird with no
tail-feathers.
Shame.

It takes bacon scraps,
potato skins, allsorts.
Favourite
is grapes.

It runs
a perfect lap of the lawn's
oval.
Give that bird a medal.

Next thing you know
you're wearing a blackbird's head,
scanning the soil.
A new god arrives

with grapes for eyes.

Phineas Gage

(1823–1860)

Railroad work, through Cavendish, Vermont.
An accidental blast: the tamping rod
enters by cheek, behind eye, comes rocketing out
the skull-top of foreman Phineas Gage,

landing behind him some thirty yards away,
a javelin greased with blood. He sits up.
Reporters note: 'Alive at 2 o'clock,
possessing all his reason, free from pain.'

Frontal brain destroyed, the healing's mixed.
His friends confess: *Gage is no longer Gage.*
Once business-like, mild-mannered, now profane,
irreverent to fellow men and God,

His work revealed by thunder, and the rod,
or living mercy—Gage remains unfixed.

Journey

The early nutter had caught his worm:
me, worn ragged with Guinness, 3 a.m.
on the last bus reserved for the head-broken.

His voices railed in concert, a paragon
of nonsense. *Duck soup! British Home Stores!* On
and on. I wished him grievous bodily harm,

all sympathy with my bearings gone
until—looking out—*there* was Orion,
disabled into stars, who was born a man . . .

I carried him with me as an arrow,
back through time, up forty miles of road,
his belt a notch off-kilter. The moon followed—

I thought of Jean-Dominique Bauby on his pillow,
paralysed except for one eyelid, slowly
winking his way towards *Fin*, his limbs in tow.

And with some bitterness I thought of you,
half-cut, dishing up your favourite quote:
A memory of love, a green meadow.

Corners came, gears moved down. By 4 a.m.
I stood in the bright vacant heart of Glasgow.

A Ring

1

You and I could be, knowing just this much—

in times of flood, clamber to the roof;
wear day-glo orange, holler. Train your sight
on tiny omens. Take them as a truth.

On orchard walls, new buds and barbed wire.
In the cat's jaws, game, as we're in love.

2

The kitchen table, the bed where we move
to serve and share the long meal of a kiss—

the lost and found debris of togetherness:
wine bottles, underwear, dead birds, amethyst—

the granny wallpaper: identical ships
on their small identical pedestals of sea.

3

With both of us asleep, the room wakes up,
a durable masque of curtains, ashtrays, cups.
They see what lies between us, face to face:

an hourglass—a space dividing profiles.

Let's taunt our eyes eternally with this,
let's always cancel one or other out.

4

Fuzzy, undefined, we look again—

our city stands, a forest of alarms,
TV aerials, dogs chewing footballs;
a broken sign which reads: *Salvation Arm.*

Invisible, the rainbow's other half,
the sister-arc that ploughs beneath the earth.

The Dancing Serpent

Charles Baudelaire

Hey lazy-bones.
I love your skin,
your velvet body's
undulating sheen.

The tang of your hair's
unfathomable waves,
blue-black and brown—
my soul wakes

to a salty morning,
pitched there, high,
a ship with its aim
on veiled skies.

Your precious eyes
neither fair nor foul,
a sub-zero blend
of gold and steel.

That easy stroll—
I see a snake,
its rhythmic lilt
upheld on a stick.

Your girlish head
lolls backwards, forwards,
blissfully heavy
as a baby elephant's.

Your body's tilt—
a slim skiff,
each flank to the slap
of water dipped.

When spittle brims
on your white teeth
like a stream swelled
by glacial melt

I'll taste it—wine,
supreme and tart,
a sky-brew splashing
my heart with *stars*.

Acoustic Mineral Wool

Insulation, sound-absorbing infill,
packed between flooring joists, partition walls.
Reduces airborne noise by ten decibels.

Impervious to vermin, non-flammable.
Does not react with wired plastic or metal
wall tiles. Growth of fungi, moulds, bacteria

not encouraged. Rot proof. Its random fibres
ensure no penetration by water.
For prices, testimonials, check our brochure:

'Silences which border on phenomenal.'
'There's no infernal knocking at the door.'
'Yes, the tigers come, but now they whisper.'

The Blue Nile

Working night and day don't make no sense . . .

A sodden June. I've collared Paul Buchanan,
blinking through a mild internal sandstorm,
and after seven years—no new album,
no artefact of commerce or devotion.

Fame-resistant, crumpled, he can say:
All I really want is an epiphany.
Behind his back, a sofa's being wheeled
the traffic-heavy length of Byres Road.

July Fugue

Not weather, but ghosts
in perpetual rotation,
great clouds of them
feeding on cherry blossom.

They share the collective
sugar memory;
the scent of ice cream
a ghost-pheromone.

In coastal towns, they comb
salt marshes for nutrients,
ply their frequencies.

At night they assemble
on rooftops, harvesting
roof-tile moss.

Who are you, then,
that I wake to at 4 a.m.,
nameless, invisible,
burned into existence,

the sheets drenched with vanilla essence.

The Temptation of Saint Anthony

And this thing dare I soothly say:
If that he were God veray,
Hunger shold greeve hym by no way;
That were against reason.

CHESTER 12: BUTCHERS

I

Fire came down. A snap. A click.
The opening and shutting of a beak.

Lightning fertilized the ground—
and so, baptized, I quit the world
to fathom God: a wilderness
lay waiting to admit my flesh.

I saw the desert scorpion, black,
fully armoured, dusting up sand
as it scuttled from under a stone, sting
erect and itching for small prey.

Whatever I turned my mind to, hatched.
For six days I fed upon the sky.

2

There is a natural surrender:
knives in a glass of clear water,

all broken by light, yet still whole.
In God's grace I break my will—
and there, upon a groaning table,
animal breeds animal

eats animal. *Creator Spiritus*,
perpetual heart of holocaust,
devotion is devouring; a flame
to spit and crackle in your name.

I make a circle here, and sit.
On brutal earth, on earth as it is—

3

The sun works on my mouth.
In prayer, words turn and taste sour.

All sense has fallen to one fact:
circulating in the bloodstream's net
a splinter of the Cross, its course
fixed blind upon my central heart.

Fever holds me high in its wings.
You my companion, architect of shadows,
tell me what appetite will serve. I know.
Your eyes are a hornets' nest of light.

The sun shakes its yellow rings.
A thorn-tree buds with gold coins.

4

The stars' mill-wheel shone.
Without warning this clear vision—

A ploughed moonlit field, a man
by jackals torn   to radiance

Bone-meal, grist, immortal soul
all fuel the furnace of the Cross

*

The desert dimmed. Rocks gave way
to gathering voices I knew and loved.
At one, delivered back to the world,
I found it very much the same.

I know the cities and their names.
A host of horn-billed angels sing.

Missing

Tell me of the scattering of the man who is saved: who are mixed with him, and who are divided from him?
ZOSTRIANOS, 45.4–5

He wanders lost in a blue
   green T-shirt and bedroom slippers
   guided by the patron saint of travellers
His printed face joins the queue at bus shelters
Seven miles from his mantelpiece he beds down
His solar-powered watch is faithful to the time
He sleeps with his head in Spain
   and his feet in Springburn
Mercury turns retrograde to Mars
At midnight he enters a market garden
   where, as prophesied, he eats
   tomatoes and strawberries
At 4 a.m. he is courted by the rain
By 6 he is pronounced in love

Saturday Night

He joined me, uninvited, at the bar: a roly-
poly dietician, his fractured jaw half bowling-ball
size and black. Over soda and lime, he gave me
his hardline battery hen philosophy:
Eating an egg is like eating a piece of Hell.

And more: the dietician had seen the Devil,
once, stepping out of a painting dressed
in sandals and a straw hat. Not only that—the Devil
followed him home and for six months hen-pecked:
Why not do yourself in. A close call. Still,

he survived. He'd had worse: like the solid hour
locked in a freighter's cold-storage compartment,
slipping on frozen kippers. Only now
he sees faces by the roadside in weeds and flowers,
my own face falling, as he rose, and simply said:

We'll meet again. I'll know where to find you.

Beast of Burden

Almanacs agree I wasn't born with it,
bending my back double. Its dead weight
constellated early: my first word, 'lumber'.

Whatever's riding my spine I see only
as it lolls or as I stumble; its nature,
always in flux, a constant mockery.

At my ear, its breath is cut grass or silage,
gardenias during summer thunder,
the scent of breast milk at room temperature.

Its beak will hoot, hoot softly. Lips flutter.
It copies my voice or a massed choir
of sea-elephants. It passes judgement.

Still barnacled there, I pray for myself
or pray to it, depending on the hour,
my skin a speckled bed of wood-skelfs.

The hill in sight, we rest, and switch our pelts.

Lauder's Bar

Sir Harry smiles from every wall.
Rain turns to sleet and falls
on three taxis planted in the rank.
A bus emblazoned *Glasgow via Reykjavik
to the USA & Canada* stands

empty opposite. Some bright spark
has amended a scrawled *UVF*
to *LOVE* in the gents' toilets.
Milling around, fake-fur coats
and shirts the colour of Opal Fruits.

Hands flare from various cuffs.
The papers are full of 'LUNAR ICE'
and far-out possibilities for life.
I'm smashed. There is no us.

Filing

Oncology Centre. Cast-iron cabinets
of case histories, fresh figures, a request
in triplicate for a 'marrow harvest'. . .
I picture a bumpkin surgeon, in a sweat,
sorting cells like apples into buckets.

Facts are sensitive here. I work my way
through bales of personal files (always 'cancer'),
my throat cracked by so much dusty paper.
Truth comes to light on X-ray:

someone's brain, a wrinkled slice of fruit;
the skull's bone, a phosphorescent hoop,
classified and coded. Someone who.

Dear X, whatever daily face you wear,
may you never falter, never flower.

The Silken Road

I take the shoots of river willow,
supple, fashioned circle-wise
and fastened so. There is a code
of charms upon the Silken Road.

They say there is a queen, her crown
a nesting-place for each cocoon:
on hatching, teams of busy worms
spin out, spin out the Silken Road.

To reach the journey's origin
brings riches . . . By this legend struck
so many homes stand empty. Miles
are posted on the Silken Road

by bones, some spread, some figuring
their common frames. That's animal,
that's other. All my brothers left
provisioned for the Silken Road,

and as I walk I scan the ground
for charcoal, tent-pegs, human tracks.
The light arches at my back
as night falls on the Silken Road.

My dream is short: a river lined
with willow, on its banks a queen
worm-eaten. There's myself grown old,
at home upon the Silken Road.

The Chemical Wedding

The hired van speeds down dual carriageways
containing us who function or don't function
as chemicals trigger off and trigger on
the infinitely occurring, infinitely dissolving images
of blown trash, tarmac, post-war brick,
the image of a wedding in the brain, seeing
our long-lost whose eyes water or remain
painfully dry, committed to their forgetting
as we are to pinning one face to one name,
the single firework of a human life, standing
still in a shower of detonated rain,
flake falling away from flake as
the one mind defoliates, flowering
down through the night air to pollinate
among leftovers of wedding cake, pink rags
of cooked ham, wrinkled balloons, beer cans,
among the assembled silences in which
there is no speech fit to be made,
while outside, on the Dublin city canal,
two snow-white midnight swans paddle by,
steer headlong through confetti, snapping bread.

In Memory of R. D. Laing

(1927–1989)

> *Painted meate no hunger feedes,*
> *Dying life each death exceeds.*
> ROBERT SOUTHWELL

The end: a simple matter. St Tropez,
cardiac arrest while playing tennis.
Our death is different, mobile, compatible
with breathing, making love or tea or money.

Two-bit dramas in ruined amphitheatres;
a sense of loss provoked by life this time.
Not to be undone, we, in our static
paradise of todays, whitewash our recent

pasts with our recent wallpaper; reduce
your passion to a comfortable cliché—
The insane are sane and vice versa?
Obvious trash. This was not your message.

You saw a man whose muscles turned to bone.
For the age, an image: petrified mass
from which the eyes stared out. With inner ground
so profitably set-aside, we work,

and every hour divine some higher purchase.
So who or what to blame? Genealogist
of pain, you hauled the Family up for trial;
you, a Protestant Scot, religion sprung

from Calvin, Luther, constipation's martyrs,
a nation stripped of saints and given *Discipline*.
Of course we weep as European walls
are broken. How could we dance? There's freedom

and there's freedom. Ours is a well-stocked fridge;
the human psyche quartered like a pie
in self-healing binges; a middle class occult.
One by one we have hijacked ourselves.

Demands? Just this: that the long not feeling
at home should end. Distance. Unbalance.
No wonder: we've placed so much faith in the air
and the air is so silent now we're so well

and truly in it, taking brief snapshots
of Earth from orbit. Earth so far from touch,
a world below that grows to nought, as systems
fail their checks, and links are lost, and we find Space.

Goodbye body. The mind's out on a limb.
What else could we do but close ranks among
mutual conspiracies of the heart,
we, the half-baked, eternal unmarried,

salvation or nemesis lying wholly
with dear ones loved to death? *Create*, you said.
And here was cause for praise: Art's descent,
unearthing the heart's apocryphal text

in Christ's long shadow, growing darker still
against our legislation of the light.
We cast our own divisions in the sun,
before, behind, within, each way we turn.

Your arrival, timed to imperfection,
was rude but not uncalled for: at best,
new sense was made; an unconditional chance
to be misunderstood beyond all guilt.

Hopefully we can return the favour,
forgive you for taking refuge in booze:
you did what any *decent* madman would,
being torn by factions, furious with God.

You wanted Him, more than most, argued
for angels in Glasgow, London, Iona.
The truth is you ran with us all, but looked back.
And we froze

Star

Home, in split seconds:
a cloudless, non-carnivorous sky,
morning star—all

I remember. As sacrifice,
this jam-jar of water
poured in the River Eden;

by Tentsmuir,
seaweed thrown to the sea.
Once more

I dream my unborn daughter:
within her palm,
one sand-grain's infinite

coastline becomes one country, becomes
the whole inhabited land.

Notes

'Night Work' is an adaptation of the untitled poem beginning 'A veces mis manos me despiertan,' included in *Vertical Poetry* by Roberto Juarroz, trans. W. S. Merwin, North Point Press, San Francisco, 1988.

'Schopenhauer's Porcupines' quotes from the song 'Can't Make a Sound' from the Elliott Smith album *Figure 8*, Dreamworks, 2000.

'X' quotes from *Looking Back at Francis Bacon* by David Sylvester, Thames and Hudson, London, 2000, and *On Jesus at Twelve Years Old*, Saint Aelred of Rievaulx, trans. Geoffrey Webb and Adrian Walker, The Saint Austin Press, London, 2001.

'Phineas Gage': for further information, see www.deakin.edu.au/hbs/gagepage/

'The Temptation of Saint Anthony' quotes from *English Mystery Plays*, ed. Peter Happé, Penguin Books, 1975.

'Missing': the quote has been slightly amended from the original translation in *The Nag Hammadi Library in English*, second edition, ed. James M. Robinson, E. J. Brill, Leiden, 1984.

'The Blue Nile' quotes from the song 'Over the Hillside' from The Blue Nile album *Hats*, Linn Records, 1989.

'In Memory of R. D. Laing' quotes from Robert Southwell, 'Marie Magdalens Complaint at Christs death,' in *The Metaphysical Poets*, revised edition, ed. Helen Gardner, Penguin Books, 1972.

For further information, visit the author's web site at www.abjackson.co.uk

Some new and recent poetry from Anvil

GAVIN BANTOCK
Just Think of It

PETER DALE
Under the Breath

DICK DAVIS
Belonging

HARRY GUEST
A Puzzling Harvest
COLLECTED POEMS 1955–2000

MICHAEL HAMBURGER
From a Diary of Non-Events

JAMES HARPUR
Oracle Bones

PHILIP HOLMES
Lighting the Steps

PETER LEVI
Viriditas

GABRIEL LEVIN
Ostraca

E A MARKHAM
A Rough Climate

SALLY PURCELL
Collected Poems

GRETA STODDART
At Home in the Dark

JULIAN TURNER
Crossing the Outskirts

DANIEL WEISSBORT
Letters to Ted